ith

Carré

Annelies Karduks

FORTE PUBLISHERS

Contents

© 2005 Forte Uitgevers, Utrecht
© 2005 for the translation by the publisher
Original title:
Elegante wenskaarten met Carré

All rights reserved.
No part of this publication may be copied, stored in an electronic file or made public, in any form or in any way whatsoever, either electronically, mechanically, by photocopying or any other form of recording, without the publisher's prior written permission.

ISBN 90 5877 631 X

This is a publication from
Forte Publishers BV
P.O. Box 1394
3500 BJ Utrecht
The Netherlands

For more information about the creative books available from Forte Uitgevers:
www.forteuitgevers.nl

Final editing: Gina Kors-Lambers, Steenwijk, the Netherlands
Photography and digital image editing: Fotografie Gerhard Witteveen, Apeldoorn, the Netherlands
Cover and inner design: BADE creatieve communicatie, Baarn, the Netherlands
Translation: Michael Ford, TextCase, Hilversum, the Netherlands

Preface	3
Techniques	4
Step-by-step	6
Materials	7
Flowers	8
Pink flowers	12
Gerberas	14
Gift cards	18
Purple flowers	20
Squirrels	24
Pink Christmas	26
Christmas	30

Preface

I have designed six new Carré templates for this second Carré book. I really enjoyed designing the cards in this book. All the pieces which are left over after making the cards in this book can be used to make your own variations.

See page 32 if you wish to remain informed of what I have in store for you in the future.

Have fun with Carré.

Annelies Karduks

Techniques

Read these instructions carefully and look at the Step-by-step photographs before you start.

It is important to always work accurately, because only then will the patterns join up nicely.

Embossing
Cut the embossing card to size (12 x 12 cm) and draw four squares (6 x 6 cm) on the back. Stick the Carré template on a light box and place the corners of the square to be embossed level with the perpendicular corners in the template. Use template tape to stick the embossing card on the template and the light box with the good side facing downwards. Emboss (part of) the pattern by going over the illuminated shapes with one of the embossing tools. To create a mirror effect, rotate the card a quarter of a revolution. If desired, use Pergasoft to make the embossing easier.

Stamp-pad ink
Applying stamp-pad ink gives the best result when you emboss first. After embossing, turn the template and the embossing card over and place them on your work surface. Use adhesive tape to cover the areas of the template which you do not wish to dab and stick the template in place. Apply stamp-pad ink to the sponge stick and dab or brush the pattern. Allow the stamp-pad ink to dry or speed up the drying process by heating the ink with a heat gun.

Cutting
Cutting is best done after you have embossed the card. After embossing, turn the template and the embossing card over, place them on your work surface and stick the template to the embossing card. Hold a sharp knife vertically and cut the lines in the template. Always cut along the same side of the cutting line. If desired, mark each part, so that you stick them on the card in the correct order.

For a square measuring 13 x 13 cm, place the outer corner of the template level with the corner of the square, stick the template it place and cut the card as described above. The outer cutting line is the line furthest away from the middle of the square. The inner cutting line is the line nearest to the middle of the square.

Tip
Almost all the cards are made with squares that measure 12 x 12 cm. If you use different colours of card, you will be left with pieces of these cards. You can use these pieces to make other cards.

Tape
Use template tape from Kars when embossing Mi-Teintes card. This tape has a layer of glue which is able to withstand the heat from a light box. However, if you must stick adhesive tape to the good side of the embossing card (for example, when dabbing stamp-pad ink and cutting the cutting lines), use 3M Scotch Removable Magic Tape. This tape has a glue layer which is not as sticky as the tape mentioned above and it is easier to remove from the embossing card. Also use this tape when embossing cArt-us card.

Use a new piece of tape for every card and save the used pieces of tape to cover the parts of the template which do not need to be coloured when applying the stamp-pad ink.

Sticking down embossed parts
Put the embossed parts through a Xyron sticker maker or use double-sided adhesive tape to stick them in place.

Attaching mini eyelets
Use a thick needle to prick holes. Place the eyelets on the thick needle, push them through the holes and use a hammer to hit the back of the eyelets flat.

Embossing with the Zip'eMate
Stick embossing card (7 x 7 cm) on the Carré template with the good side facing downwards. Make sure that the template tape does not go over the embossing patterns in the template on both sides. Stick the following things on top of each other: the basic plate for the punches, the Carré template with the card on top, the black embossing foam (allow more than 1 cm to protrude from the rear) and the embossing mat with the sloping edges facing upwards. Next, put all of this through the Zip'eMate. If the embossing is not deep enough, rotate the template and the card a quarter of a revolution, place the transparent shim sheet under the Carré template and put everything through the Zip'eMate again.

Step-by-step

1. Embossing and rotating the embossing card.

2. Applying stamp-pad ink.

3. Cutting.

4. Making the various parts into a card.

Materials

- *Card and paper: cArt-us, Mi-Teintes Canson, Papicolor (P) and Bazzill Basics (the colour numbers are given with the instructions)*
- *Carré templates C01, C02, C03, C11 C12, C13, C21, C22, C23, C31, C32, C33*
- *Scoring pen*
- *Cutting ruler with a metal edge*
- *Cutting mat*
- *Hobby knife*
- *Tweezer scissors*
- *Template tape*
- *3M Scotch Removable Magic Tape*
- *3D cutting sheets*
- *Photographs*
- *Photo glue*
- *Double-sided adhesive foil*
- *Xyron 250 with permanent cartridge*
- *3D foam blocks and/or silicon glue*
- *Light box*
- *Fiskars embossing tool (small tip)*
- *Fiskars embossing tool (regular tip)*
- *Eyelet toolset*
- *Eyelet hammer*
- *Needle*
- *Propelling pencil*
- *Rubber*
- *Stamp-pad ink*
- *Sponge sticks*
- *Heat gun*

Flowers

Poppies

What you need
- cArt-us card: yellow 275 (P 28)
- Mi-Teintes card: white 335 (P 30) and apple green 475 (P 169)
- Carré template: C 33
- Picturel cutting sheet: anemone and poppy (1036)
- Zip'eMate

Instructions

1. Cut, score and fold a yellow double card (13.5 x 13.5 cm). Place the outer corner of the template in the corner of the card, cut both cutting lines and cut out the piece of card. Do this in all the corners. Cut a white square (12 x 12 cm) and five apple green squares (one of 13.4 x 13.4 cm and four of 7 x 7 cm).

2. Look at the photograph to see which part of the pattern is to be left out and how the white square must be placed on the template. Emboss the pattern four times. Cut the inner cutting lines four times.

3. Stick the good side of the apple green square on the template and put it through the Zip'eMate. Emboss the sections. Do this for all the green squares and cut the corners off.

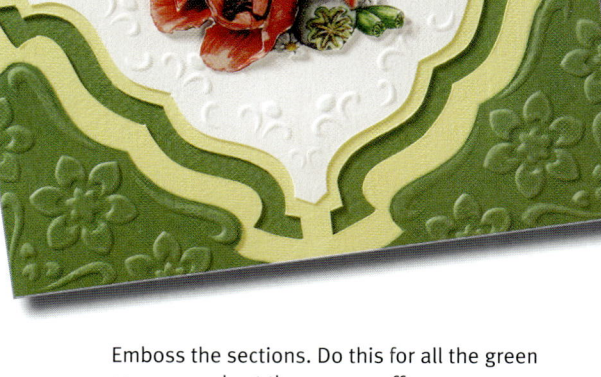

4. Stick everything on and in the card. Make the poppies 3D.

Happy Birthday

What you need
- cArt-us card: yellow 275 (P 28)
- Mi-Teintes card: white 335 (P 30) and apple green 475 (P 169)
- Carré template: C 32
- Megumi punch sheet: anemone 05
- Text Charms
- Mini eyelets: assorted primary colours

Instructions

1. Cut, score and fold a yellow double card (13.5 x 13.5 cm). Cut a white square (12 x 12 cm) and an apple green square (13 x 13 cm).

2. Look at the photograph to see which part of the pattern is to be left out and how the white square must be placed on the template. Emboss the pattern four times. Cut the inner cutting lines four times. Cut the shape in two.

3. Stick the template on the apple green square and cut the inner cutting lines four times. Cut the shape in two.

4. Stick all the parts on the card. Add the text charm and the eyelets. Make the flowers 3D.

Peonies

What you need
- cArt-us card: yellow 275 (P 28)
- Mi-Teintes card: white 335 (P 30) and apple green 475 (P 169)
- Carré template: C 31
- Picturel cutting sheet: anemone and poppy (1036)
- Brads: flower aquarelle

Instructions

1. Cut, score and fold a yellow double card (13.5 x 13.5 cm). Cut a white square (12 x 12 cm) and an apple green square (12.4 x 12.4 cm).

2. Look at the photograph to see which part of the pattern is to be left out and how the white square must be placed on the template. Emboss the pattern four times. Cut both cutting lines four times.

3. Stick everything on the card. Add the Brads. Make the flowers 3D.

Yellow Christmas rose

Instructions
1. Cut, score and fold an apple green double card (13.5 x 13.5 cm). Cut a white square (12 x 12 cm) and an yellow square (13 x 13 cm).

2. Look at the photograph to see which part of the pattern is to be left out and how the white square must be placed on the template C 12. Emboss the pattern four times. Cut the outer cutting lines four times.

3. Stick template C 02 on the yellow square and cut the inner cutting lines four times.

4. Stick all the parts on the card. Use line stickers and corner stickers to decorate the card. Add the Brads. Make the Christmas rose 3D.

What you need
- cArt-us card: yellow 275 (P 28)
- Mi-Teintes card: white 335 (P 30) and apple green 475 (P 169)
- Carré templates: C 02 and C 12
- Megumi punch sheet: yellow Christmas rose (04)
- Gold line stickers and corner stickers
- Flower Brads: monochromatic green

Pink flowers

Amaryllis

What you need
- *Bazzill card: flamingo 131 (P 15), watermelon 222 (P 33) and maraschino 250 (P 43)*
- *Mi-Teintes card: white 335 (P 30)*
- *Carré templates: C 13 and C 32*
- *Picturel cutting sheet: amaryllis frame (1057)*

Instructions

1. Cut, score and fold a pale red double card (13.5 x 13.5 cm). Cut a dark red square (13 x 13 cm), a mid-red square (12 x 12 cm) and a white square (12 x 12 cm).

2. Look at the photograph to see which part of the pattern is to be left out and how the white square must be placed on the template C 32. Emboss the pattern four times. Cut the outer cutting lines four times.

3. Stick template C 32 on the mid-red square and cut the inner cutting lines four times. Stick template C 13 on the dark red square and cut the inner cutting lines four times.

4. Stick all the parts on the card. Make the amaryllis 3D.

12

Rose

What you need
- Bazzill card: watermelon 222 (P 33) and maraschino 250 (P 43)
- Mi-Teintes card: white 335 (P 30)
- Carré templates: C 13 and C 33
- Picturel cutting sheet: Christmas rose diamond (1052)
- Eyelets: assorted soft aquarelle

Instructions

1. Cut, score and fold a mid-red double card (13.5 x 13.5 cm). Cut a dark red square (13 x 13 cm) and a white square (12 x 12 cm).

2. Look at the photograph to see which part of the pattern is to be left out and how the white square must be placed on the template C 33. Emboss the pattern four times. Cut the outer cutting lines four times.

3. Stick template C 13 on the dark red square and cut the inner cutting lines four times.

4. Stick all the parts on the card and add the eyelets. Make the rose 3D.

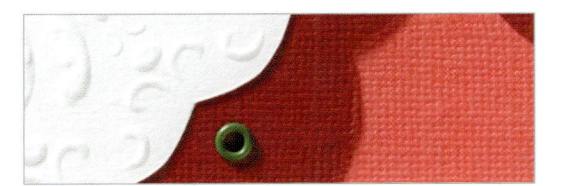

Gerberas

Purple gerbera

What you need
- cArt-us card: dark green 309 (P 18) and spring green 305 (P 08)
- Mi-Teintes card: white 335 (P 30)
- Carré templates: C 01 and C 31
- Shake-it cutting sheet: gerberas (IT 421)
- Stamp-pad ink: lime
- Sponge stick
- Line stickers

Instructions
1. Cut, score and fold a dark green double card (13.5 x 13.5 cm). Cut a white square (12 x 12 cm) and a spring green square (12 x 12 cm).

2. Look at the photograph to see which part of the pattern is to be left out and how the white square must be placed on the template C 31. Emboss the pattern four times. Apply stamp-pad ink to some of the embossed parts and allow it to dry. Cut the outer cutting lines four times.

3. Stick template C 01 on the spring green square and cut both cutting lines four times.

4. Stick all the parts on the card. Use line stickers to decorate the card. Make the gerbera 3D.

Pink gerbera

Instructions
1. Cut, score and fold a spring green double card (10.5 x 14.8 cm). Cut out two dark green squares (6 x 6 cm) and two white squares (6 x 6 cm).

2. Emboss both white squares by placing the corners level with the perpendicular corners in the template. Cut the cutting line which is closest to the embossed part.

3. Cut both dark green squares by placing the corners level with the perpendicular corners in the template. Cut the other cutting line.

4. Stick all the parts on the card. Add the text Charm and the eyelets. Make the gerbera 3D.

What you need
- cArt-us card: dark green 309 (P 18) and spring green 305 (P 08)
- Mi-Teintes card: white 335 (P 30)
- Carré template: C 32
- Shake-it cutting sheet: gerberas (IT 421)
- Mini eyelets: assorted clear aquarelle
- Text Charms
- Brads: silver, round
- Silver line stickers

White gerbera

What you need
- cArt-us card: dark green 309 (P 18) and spring green 305 (P 08)
- Mi-Teintes card: white 335 (P 30)
- Carré template: C 11
- Shake-it cutting sheet: gerberas (IT 421)
- Mini adhesive stones: white

Instructions
1. Cut, score and fold a dark green double card (10.5 x 14.8 cm). Cut a spring green square (13 x 13 cm) and two white squares (6 x 6 cm).

2. Emboss both white squares by placing the corners level with the perpendicular corners in the template. Cut the cutting line which is closest to the embossed part.

3. Place the outer corner of the template level with the corner of the spring green square. Cut both cutting lines in two opposite corners and cut out the shape 0.5 cm from the edge. Cut only the inner cutting lines in the other corners.

4. Stick the embossed parts on the spring green square and stick this square on the card at an angle. Carefully cut off the protruding parts along the edge of the card. Use adhesive stones to decorate the card. Make the gerbera 3D.

Gerbera with Brads

Instructions

1. Cut, score and fold a dark green double card (13.5 x 13.5 cm). Cut a white square (12 x 12 cm) and a spring green square (13 x 13 cm).

2. Look at the photograph to see which part of the pattern is to be left out and how the white square must be placed on the template C 31. Emboss the pattern four times. Cut both cutting lines four times.

3. Stick template C 32 on the spring green square and cut the inner cutting lines four times.

4. Stick all the parts on the card. Add the Brads. Make the gerbera 3D.

What you need
- cArt-us card: dark green 309 (P 18) and spring green 305 (P 08)
- Mi-Teintes card: white 335 (P 30)
- Carré templates: C 31 and C 32
- Shake-it cutting sheet: gerberas (IT 421)
- Flower Brads: monochromatic green

Gift cards

Purple flowers

What you need
- cArt-us card: dark blue 417 (P 41) and lilac 453 (P 14)
- Mi-Teintes card: white 335 (P 30)
- Carré template: C 32
- Shake-it cutting sheet: small anemones and gerberas (IT 426)
- Snaps: transparent colours - small
- Snaps: pastel colours - small

Instructions
1. Cut, score and fold a dark blue double card (7 x 7 cm). Cut a lilac square (6.6 x 6.6 cm) and a white square (6.2 x 6.2 cm).

2. Emboss the white square by placing the corners level with the perpendicular corners in the template. Emboss the pattern four times.

3. Stick everything on the card and add the Snaps. Make the flower 3D.

Red flowers

What you need
- cArt-us card: dark blue 417 (P 41) and old red 517 (P 12)
- Mi-Teintes card: white 335 (P 30)
- Carré templates: C 31 and C 33
- Shake-it cutting sheet: small anemones and gerberas (IT 426)
- Snaps: primary colours - small
- Mini eyelets: primary colours

Instructions
1. Cut, score and fold a dark blue double card (7 x 7 cm). Cut an old red square (6.6 x 6.6 cm) and a white square (6.2 x 6.2 cm).

2. Emboss the white square by placing the corners level with the perpendicular corners in the template. Emboss the pattern four times.

3. Stick everything on the card and add the Snaps and the eyelets. Make the flower 3D.

Purple flowers

Hydrangeas

What you need
- *Bazzill card: wisteria 620 (P 37) and forget-me-not 638 (P 46)*
- *Mi-Teintes card: white 335 (P 30)*
- *Carré template: C 33*
- *Photograph*

Instructions

1. Cut, score and fold a pale purple double card (10.5 x 14.8 cm). Cut a mid-purple square (13 x 13 cm) and two white squares (6 x 6 cm).

2. Emboss both white squares by placing the corners level with the perpendicular corners in the template. Cut the cutting line which is closest to the embossed part.

3. Draw a diagonal cross on the back of the photograph. Place the perpendicular corner in the template (with the flower in the middle) level with where the lines cross. Cut the inner cutting line four times. Place the outer corner of the template level with the corner of the mid-purple square. Cut the outer cutting line in two opposite corners and cut out the shape 0.5 cm from the edge.

4. Stick the photograph and the embossed parts on the mid-purple square. Stick this square on the card at an angle. Carefully cut off the protruding parts along the edge of the card.

Columnines

What you need
- Bazzill card: wisteria 620 (P 37) and forget-me-not 638 (P 46)
- Mi-Teintes card: white 335 (P 30)
- Carré template: C 03
- Photograph
- Stamp-pad ink: heliotrope
- Sponge stick

Instructions

1. Cut, score and fold a pale purple double card (10.5 x 14.8 cm). Cut a mid-purple rectangle (9.5 x 13.8 cm), cut the photograph so that it measures 8.5 x 12.8 cm and cut two white squares (6 x 6 cm).

2. Emboss both white squares by placing the corners level with the perpendicular corners in the template. Apply stamp-pad ink to the embossed parts and allow it to dry. Cut the cutting line which is closest to the embossed part.

3. Cut the photograph by placing the corners level with the perpendicular corners in the template. Cut the other cutting line.

4. Stick all the parts on the card.

Chrysanthemums

What you need
- *Bazzill card: wisteria 620 (P 37) and pansy 640*
- *Mi-Teintes card: white 335 (P 30)*
- *Carré templates: C 31 and C 33*
- *Megumi cutting sheet: chrysanthemum 06*
- *Stamp-pad ink: heliotrope*
- *Sponge stick*

Instructions
1. Cut, score and fold a pale purple double card (13.5 x 13.5 cm). Cut a dark purple square (13 x 13 cm) and a white square (12 x 12 cm).

2. Look at the photograph to see which part of the pattern is to be left out and how the white square must be placed on the template C 33. Emboss the pattern four times. Apply stamp-pad ink to some of the embossed parts and allow it to dry. Cut both cutting lines four times.

3. Stick template C 31 on the dark purple square and cut the inner cutting lines four times.

4. Stick all the parts on the card. Make the chrysanthemums 3D.

Hibiscus

Instructions

1. Cut, score and fold a pale purple double card (13.5 x 13.5 cm). Cut a mid-purple square (13 x 13 cm) and a dark purple square (13 x 13 cm).

2. Look at the photograph to see which part of the pattern is to be left out and how the white square must be placed on the template C 32. Emboss the pattern four times. Cut the outer cutting lines four times.

3. Stick template C 32 on the mid-purple square and cut the inner cutting lines four times. Stick template C 32 on the dark purple square and cut the inner cutting lines four times.

4. Stick all the parts on the card. Add the Brads. Make the flowers 3D.

What you need

- *Bazzill card: wisteria 620 (P 37), forget-me-not 638 (P 46) and pansy 640*
- *Mi-Teintes card: white 335 (P 30)*
- *Carré templates: C 32 and C 03*
- *Nel van Veen cutting sheet: exotic flowers (6003)*
- *Flower Brads: monochromatic purple*

Squirrels

On the rocks

What you need
- cArt-us card: terracotta 549 (P 35) and ochre 575 (P 26)
- Mi-Teintes card: white 335 (P 30)
- Carré template: C 33
- Photograph
- Brads: flower monochromatic orange

Instructions
1. Cut, score and fold an ochre double card (10.5 x 14.8 cm). Cut a terracotta rectangle (10 x 14.3 cm), cut the photograph so that it measures 9.5 x 13.8 cm and cut two white squares (6 x 6 cm).

2. Emboss both white squares by placing the corners level with the perpendicular corners in the template. Cut the cutting line which is closest to the embossed part.

3. Cut the photograph by placing the corners level with the perpendicular corners in the template. Cut the other cutting line.

4. Stick all the parts on the card. Add the Brads.

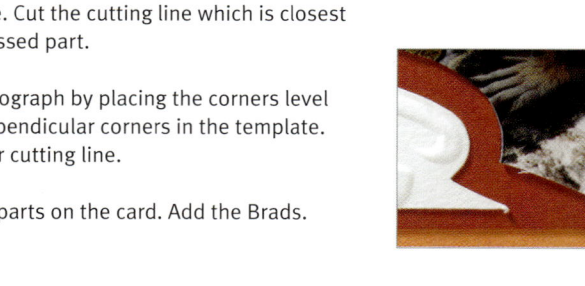

On a tree trunk

Instructions
1. Cut, score and fold an ochre double card (13.5 x 13.5 cm). Cut two terracotta squares (13 x 13 cm and 6.5 x 6.5 cm), an ochre square (9.5 x 9.5 cm) and two white squares (12.5 x 12.5 cm and 9 x 9 cm). Cut the photograph so that it measures 6 x 6 cm.

2. Emboss both white squares by placing the corners level with the perpendicular corners in the template. Emboss the pattern eight times. Pay attention to which sections of the pattern are used.

3. Stick all the squares on the card and add the eyelets.

What you need
- cArt-us card: terracotta 549 (P 35) and ochre 575 (P 26)
- Mi-Teintes card: white 335 (P 30)
- Carré template: C 32
- Photograph
- Eyelets: monochromatic orange

Pink Christmas

Pinecone

What you need
- cArt-us card: dark red 519 (P 43), warm pink 485 (P 33) and pink 481 (P 34)
- Papicolor Brilliant: gravel (P 161)
- Carré template: C 21
- Picturel cutting sheet: Christmas rose frame (1056)
- Mini adhesive stones: light green
- Zip'eMate

Instructions
1. Cut, score and fold a dark red double card (13.5 x 13.5 cm). Place the outer corner of the template in the corner of the card, cut both cutting lines and cut out the piece of card. Do this in all the corners. Cut a gravel square (12 x 12 cm), a pale pink square (13.4 x 13.4 cm) and four warm pink squares (7 x 7 cm).

2. Look at the photograph to see which part of the pattern is to be left out and how the gravel square must be placed on the template. Emboss the pattern four times. Cut the inner cutting lines four times.

3. Stick the good side of the warm pink green square on the template and put it through the Zip'eMate. Do this for all the warm pink squares and cut the corners off.

4. Stick all the parts on the card. Stick the Christmas rose and the pinecone on the card and make them 3D.

Hellebore

What you need
- cArt-us card: dark red 519 (P 43) and warm pink 485 (P 33)
- Papicolor Brilliant: gravel (P 161)
- Carré templates: C 22 and C 23
- Nel van Veen cutting sheet: small hellebore (2254)
- Eyelets: monochromatic green

Instructions
1. Cut, score and fold a dark red double card (13.5 x 13.5 cm). Cut a warm pink square (13 x 13 cm) and two gravel squares (12 x 12 cm).

2. Look at the photograph to see which part of the pattern is to be left out and how the gravel square must be placed on the template C 22. Emboss the pattern four times. Cut the inner cutting lines four times. Look at the photograph to see which part of the pattern is to be left out and how the gravel square must be placed on the template C 23. Emboss the pattern four times. Cut the outer cutting lines four times.

3. Stick template C 22 on the warm pink square and cut both cutting lines four times.

4. Stick all the parts on the card and add the eyelets. Stick the hellebore on the card and make it 3D.

Pink flowers

What you need
- *cArt-us card: dark red 519 (P 43) and warm pink 485 (P 33)*
- *Papicolor Brilliant: gravel (P 161)*
- *Carré templates: C 21 and C 23*
- *Megumi punch sheet: Christmas rose red (01)*
- *Eyelets: monochromatic green*

Instructions

1. Cut, score and fold a dark red double card (13.5 x 13.5 cm). Cut a warm pink square (13 x 13 cm) and two gravel squares (12 x 12 cm).

2. Look at the photograph to see which part of the pattern is to be left out and how the gravel square must be placed on the template C 21. Emboss the pattern four times. Cut the inner cutting lines four times.

3. Look at the photograph to see which part of the pattern is to be left out and how the gravel square must be placed on the template C 23. Emboss the pattern four times. Cut the outer cutting lines four times. Stick template C 21 on the warm pink square and cut the outer cutting lines four times.

4. Stick all the parts on the card and add the eyelets. Stick the picture of the pink flowers on the card and make it 3D.

Christmas bells

What you need
- cArt-us card: dark red 519 (P 43) and warm pink 485 (P 33)
- Papicolor Brilliant: gravel (P 161)
- Carré template: C 22
- Picturel cutting sheet: Christmas rose frame (1056)

Instructions

1. Cut, score and fold a warm pink double card (13.5 x 13.5 cm). Cut a dark red square (12.5 x 12.5 cm), a warm pink square (13 x 13 cm) and a gravel square (12 x 12 cm).

2. Look at the photograph to see which part of the pattern is to be left out and how the gravel square must be placed on the template. Emboss the pattern four times. Cut the outer cutting lines four times.

3. Stick the template on the warm pink square and cut both cutting lines four times.

4. Stick all the parts on the card. Stick the picture of a Christmas rose with bells on the card and make it 3D.

Christmas

Christmas rose

What you need
- cArt-us card: old red 517 (P 12) and dark green 309 (P 18)
- Papicolor Brilliant: cream 163
- Carré template: C 22
- Marjoleine cutting sheet: Christmas roses
- Stamp-pad ink: pheasant gold
- Sponge stick
- Snaps: primary colours - small

Instructions

1. Cut, score and fold an old red double card (13.5 x 13.5 cm). Cut three dark green squares (12.5 x 12.5 cm, 9.5 x 9.5 cm and 6.5 x 6.5 cm) and two cream squares (12 x 12 cm and 9 x 9 cm).

2. Emboss both cream squares by placing the corners level with the perpendicular corners in the template. Emboss the pattern eight times. Apply stamp-pad ink to some of the embossed parts and allow it to dry.

3. Stick all the parts on the card and add the Snaps. Make the Christmas rose 3D.

Christmas roses

What you need
- cArt-us card: old red 517 (P 12) and dark green 309 (P 18)
- Papicolor Brilliant: cream 163
- Carré templates: C 21 and C 22
- Megumi punch sheet: Christmas red (01)
- Border stickers: transparent flowers - gold

Instructions
1. Cut, score and fold an old red double card (13.5 x 13.5 cm). Cut a dark green square (13 x 13 cm) and a cream square (12 x 12 cm).

2. Look at the photograph to see which part of the pattern is to be left out and how the cream square must be placed on the template C 21. Emboss the pattern four times. Cut both cutting lines four times.

3. Stick template C 22 on the dark green square and cut the inner cutting lines four times.

4. Stick all the parts on the card. Use sticker dots to decorate the card. Stick the picture of Christmas roses on the card and make it 3D.

Snowman

What you need
- Bazzill card: jacaranda (707) and arctic (708)
- Mi-Teintes card: azure 102 (P 19)
- Carré template: C 23
- Marjoleine cutting sheet: snowmen
- Stamp-pad ink: royal blue
- Sponge stick
- Snaps: primary colours - small

Instructions

1. Cut, score and fold a mid-blue double card (13.5 x 13.5 cm). Cut two dark blue squares (13 x 13 cm and 4.8 x 4.8 cm) and an azure square (12 x 12 cm).

2. Look at the photograph to see which part of the pattern is to be left out and how the azure square must be placed on the template. Emboss the pattern four times. Apply stamp-pad ink to some of the embossed parts and allow it to dry. Cut both cutting lines four times.

3. Stick all the parts on the card and add the Snaps. Stick the snowman on the card and make it 3D.

Many thanks to Kars & Co. B.V. in Ochten, the Netherlands, and craft shop Crealies in Amersfoort, the Netherlands, for providing the materials. Shopkeepers can order the materials from Kars & Co B.V. and Papicolor. Card-makers can order the materials from craft shop Crealies, Anna Boelensgaarde 23, 3824 BR Amersfoort, the Netherlands, +31 (0)33 4564052 (until 6 p.m.). The shop is open on appointment. E-mail: info@crealies.nl. Also see www.crealies.nl. If you wish to remain informed about what I have in store for you in the future, then complete the form on the website.